SHAKER BOY

SHAKER BOY

BY Mary Lyn Ray

ILLUSTRATED BY Jeanette Winter

Browndeer Press
Harcourt Brace & Company
SAN DIEGO   NEW YORK   LONDON

For Bill
— M. L. R.

Text copyright © 1994 by Mary Lyn Ray
Illustrations copyright © 1994 by Jeanette Winter

Requests for permission to make copies of any part of the work should be mailed to:
Permissions Department, Harcourt Brace & Company,
6277 Sea Harbor Drive, Orlando, Florida 32887-6777.

The following songs — "Love is little," "I have a little noggin," "A little voice is heard to
say," and "The heavens are with us" — are from Daniel W. Patterson, *The Shaker Spiritual*,
copyright © 1979 by Princeton University Press. Reprinted by permission of
Princeton University Press.

The following songs — "More love," "Low, low," and "O this pretty little trumpet" —
are from Edward Deming Andrews, *The Gift To Be Simple,* Dover Publications Inc.
Used by permission.

Library of Congress Cataloging-in-Publication Data
Ray, Mary Lyn.
Shaker boy/by Mary Lyn Ray; illustrated by Jeanette Winter. — 1st ed.
p.   cm.
"Browndeer Press."
Summary: Having come to live among the Shakers at the age of six,
Caleb spends the rest of his life learning their songs and their ways.
ISBN 0-15-276921-8
[1. Shakers — Fiction.] I. Winter, Jeanette, ill. II. Title.
PZ7.R210154Sh   1994
[E] — dc20   93-1333

Printed in Singapore
First edition   A B C D E

PRINTED IN SINGAPORE

The illustrations in this book were done in acrylics on Strathmore Bristol.
The text type was set in Bembo by Thompson Type, San Diego, California.
Hand-lettering and music calligraphed by Judythe Sieck
Color separations were made by Bright Arts, Ltd., Singapore.
Printed and bound by Tien Wah Press, Singapore
This book was printed with soya-based inks on Leykam
recycled paper, which contains more than 20 percent postconsumer
waste and has a total recycled content of at least 50 percent.
Production supervision by Warren Wallerstein and Ginger Boyer
Design by Trina Stahl and Judythe Sieck

Author's Note

The Shaker experiment in religious community, which began in England, was brought to America in 1774 by a small group of pilgrims and their founder, Ann Lee (1736–84). By the middle of the nineteenth century, there were eleven Shaker villages in New England and New York, and seven others to the west. Then gradually membership declined. The only surviving community of Shakers is at Sabbathday Lake, Maine. However, many of the villages, including the one at Canterbury, New Hampshire, are open as museums.

Much about the Shakers was radical. In a time when women in America had few legal rights, the Shakers treated men and women equally. For every male position of authority, there was a corresponding female one, and all decisions in a community were made by both the male and female leaders. Property was owned jointly by the members of a community, and all responsibilities were shared. In everything they did — even the humblest tasks — the Shakers pledged "to improve their time and talents in the way that would be most useful." Work was regarded as worship.

Although the Shakers chose to live apart from what they called the world, they were some of the most progressive people of their day. Always looking for a better way, they experimented with advanced systems of farming, manufacturing, and selling. Radical, too, in welcoming all races and nationalities, the Shakers taught kindness, generosity, and peace. Members lived a life of simplicity and economy. Although their lives appeared strict and severe to outsiders, they knew much joy and beauty.

Marriage was not permitted in a Shaker community. But the Shakers had deep love of children and took in any who needed homes. When they were older, some of the children returned to "the world"; others chose to remain with their Shaker families.

When Caleb Whitcher came to live with the Shakers, he suddenly acquired 141 brothers and 138 sisters. He had never seen such an unusual family, or such an unusual house. It had 162 rooms. One side was for the men; the other side was for the women.

Children lived in a separate house until they turned
thirteen. Then they moved to the big house.

   Beyond the house were other big, square buildings,
and beyond them only sky. No place was whiter or
quieter than their village. The Shakers called it Holy
Ground because they said angels were near.

Caleb was six years old. When his father was killed in
the Civil War, his mother sold their farm and went to
Lowell to work in the mills. But the mills were no
place for a boy, she said, and she left Caleb with the
Shakers at Canterbury, New Hampshire.

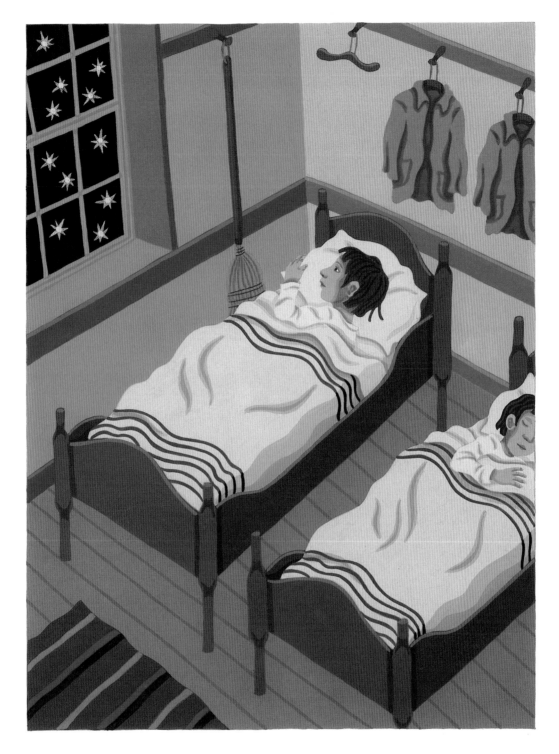

The Shakers all called God their "father" and a woman named Ann "mother." They dressed alike, slept in beds alike, sat straight in chairs alike, shared all they owned alike, and all alike loved God and Mother Ann.

Caleb was deciding whether he liked the Shakers when he heard a little song.

He was sure he heard it. But there was no one singing. A brother said it must be an angel.

Caleb didn't believe it, but he saw that the Shakers believed. "If thee minds Mother, she will show thee the angels," they said.

A lit~tle voice is heard to say, Come fol~low me; this is the way. My lit~tle flock I will con~vey, By lit~tle steps ad~vanc~ing. 'Tis Moth~er bids her chil~dren come, And feeds them with the heav'n~ly crumb; The Fath~er greets them wel~come home, With mus~ic and with danc~ing danc~ing.

It wasn't always easy, minding. The Shakers had rules unnatural for boys.

"Thee must not rest thy feet on the rungs of thy chair, nor tilt back for thy comfort."

"Order is the first law of heaven and the salvation of souls."

"Thee must surrender thy will and go or come when called."

But there was one rule Caleb liked. All the sisters and
brothers were expected to Shaker their plates. They
had to eat whatever was served them because it was
wrong to let anything waste.

Apple pie appeared at almost every meal, and Caleb
thought it no burden to Shaker it.

When Caleb attended Sunday meeting, he learned where the name Shaker came from. For a while the brothers and sisters sat solemn and still, until suddenly

they stood and shook. "To shake out Old Ugly," they said. Then they began to dance, because now they were limber and free.

Usually they met in the meetinghouse. But sometimes
they marched to a place in the woods they considered
especially holy.

The only music was their singing. It made Caleb think of bees in the blooms of apples in May.

Sometimes in meeting, Caleb and the children were given pretend toys. Caleb imagined balls, boats, horns, and drums. Each came with a little song.

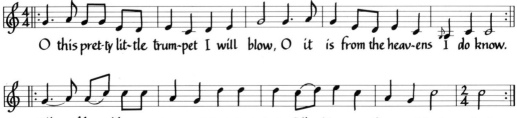

O this pret-ty lit-tle trum-pet I will blow, O it is from the heav-ens I do know.

I'll blow, blow my trum-pet, toot, toot, toot, I'll blow my trum-pet, toot, toot.

The Shakers didn't believe in real toys. But they believed in school.

Classes were held three months in summer for the girls and three months in winter for the boys.

Caleb looked out at drifting snow while he read about elephants in India. Most of what he learned, he learned outside school.

When morning was still dark, the bell on the big house rang to call the Shakers to work. Everyone had a job; the smallest had the smallest jobs. Caleb went to the hen house. The sisters in the kitchen needed 280 eggs for breakfast.

Then he fed and watered the chickens and sang them an angel song.

I have a lit~ tle nog~ gin full of Love sweet Love Love.

Moth~ er sent me here with it To feed her sim~ ple Doves.

It is sweet it is sweet, It is ver~ y sweet Chick, chick

chick chick pret~ ty chicks come and eat

All day, all year, Caleb helped the brothers. There were always errands between the mills and shops and barns.

When he was older and his hands had grown some, Caleb learned to milk Old Jewel. Each boy over eight had the care of a cow in the big, big cow barn.

In the broom shop Caleb learned to make the flat brooms
Shakers had invented. In one winter he made 2,620.

When he worked at the mill, turning handles, he held
long shavings to his chin, pretending to be an old man
with an old beard.

Once the angels taught him a broom song.

Low, low! Low, low! In this pret-ty path I will go, For here Moth-er leads me and I know it is right. I will sweep as I go, I will sweep as I go, For this Moth-er bids me and it is my de~ light.

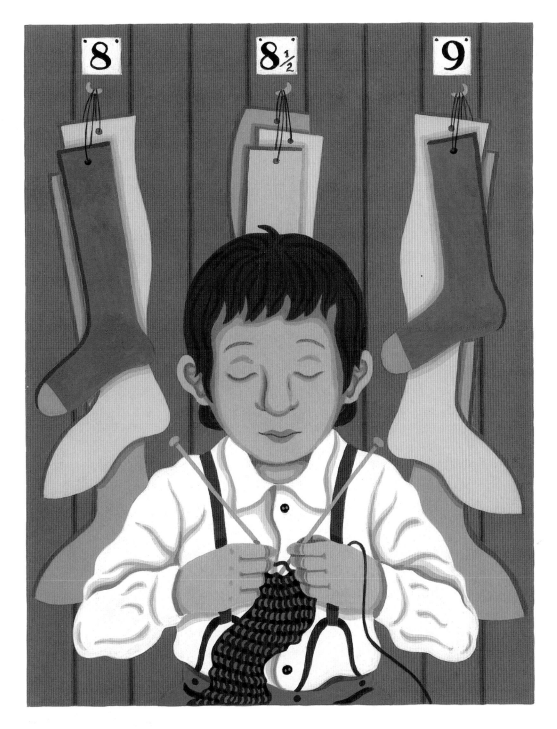

Some days Caleb rode to Concord or Laconia to deliver brooms and other articles the brothers made for sale.

Some days he knitted socks, or helped mend coffeepots and milk pans in the tin shop.

"When thee grows an inch, thee grows another talent," Elder Henry told him.

As winter passed, nights stayed cold but days began to warm. Sap ran in the maples and sugaring began. Boys carried buckets to the trees and watched for them to fill. They had supper at the camp and were allowed to spend the night.

Sap was cooked down to syrup, and syrup was cooked down to sugar. The men took turns boiling the sap and sleeping. The boys did not sleep at all.

Only Caleb heard songs in the flickering coals.

Love is lit~tle, love is low Love will make my spir~it grow.

Grow in peace, grow in light Love will do the thing that's right

When sugaring was done, the brothers prepared the fields for planting. Caleb had to pick stones, a job he did not enjoy.

"Thee must respect the stones," said Brother Otis, who laid the long, level stone walls. "There is a place for everything." But Caleb noticed that the angels never sang a stone song.

Summer was a growing time, a good time — Caleb
thought — to graze like Old Jewel in the tall grass.

But there was always something a boy was wanted for.

One year the captain of the steamer *Lady of the Lake* invited all the Shakers for a holiday on the great Winnipesaukee. The invitation was accepted, and every kind of vehicle the family had was reserved for transportation. Even then not everyone could go.

Too soon, maples in the swamps turned red. Summer's last mowing began.

For days Caleb and the younger boys raked and cocked the windrows, while the older brothers carted to the barn what they had cut the day before.

After the hay was in, there was corn to shuck. There
were potatoes to dig and apples to pick and store and
press for cider. Early fall Caleb and the brothers began
to cut stove wood to be used the next year.

After snow they sledded the logs from the woodlots
and piled them at the sawmill, where they cut them to
stove length and split them. Then the boys filled the
woodshed — five hundred cords each year.

When Caleb was thirteen, he moved to the big house.
That night he began a journal: "I am surely beginning
to be a man."

In the print shop he learned to set type. When he had free time, he printed the songs he had heard and sewed them into a book.

More love, more love; The heav-ens are bless-ing, The an- gels are
More love, more love. A- lone by its pow-er The world we will

call-ing, O Zi- on, more love. If ye love not each oth- er in dai- ly com-
con-quer For true love is God. If ye love one an- oth- er, Then God dwell-eth

mun- ion, How can ye love God, Whom ye have not seen?
in you, And ye are made strong, To live by His word.

When he was nineteen, Caleb was made deacon of the apple orchard.

Every year he supervised the planting and pruning and picking and storing, the making of sauce and cider.

One day Elder Henry came to Caleb in the orchard and showed him a tree he had never seen. When the wind blew the leaves, the tree sang.

Elder Henry said to Caleb, "Thee shall have care of the Tree of Songs and gather for us the prettiest."

And he did.

Every day Caleb went to the orchard. Sometimes he picked apples.

Sometimes he picked songs.

And when he was an old, old man, he saw the angels.

The heav~ens are with us I know. [Rich] treas~ures like riv~ers do flow. I feel all that's earth~ly is pass~ing a~way And I'm tast~ing of glo~ries im~mor~tal. Bright An~gels a~round us do hov~er, With heal~ing our wounds they would cov~er, And they would waft, waft, waft our spir~its from toil and vex~a~tion to live in their un~ion for~ev~er.